MILES MORALES:

WRITER: **BRIAN MICHAEL BENDIS**

ARTIST: **SARA PICHELLI**

FINISHES, ISSUE #5: **DAVID MESSINA**

COLORIST: **JUSTIN PONSOR**

LETTERER: **VC'S CORY PETIT**

COVER ART: **KAARE ANDREWS**

ULTIMATE COMICS FALLOUT #4

REED RICHARDS

    WRITER: **JONATHAN HICKMAN**

    ARTIST: **SALVADOR LARROCA**

    COLORIST: **FRANK D'ARMATA**

VALERIE COOPER

    WRITER: **NICK SPENCER**

    ARTIST: **CLAYTON CRAIN**

LETTERERS: **VC'S CORY PETIT & CLAYTON COWLES**

COVER ART: **MARK BAGLEY, ANDY LANNING & JUSTIN PONSOR**

ASSISTANT EDITOR: **JON MOISAN**

ASSOCIATE EDITOR: **SANA AMANAT**

SENIOR EDITOR: **MARK PANICCIA**

SPIDER-MAN CREATED BY **STAN LEE & STEVE DITKO**

COLLECTION EDITOR: **JENNIFER GRÜNWALD**

ASSISTANT EDITOR: **CAITLIN O'CONNELL**

ASSOCIATE MANAGING EDITOR: **KATERI WOODY**

EDITOR, SPECIAL PROJECTS: **MARK D. BEAZLEY**

VP PRODUCTION & SPECIAL PROJECTS: **JEFF YOUNGQUIST**

SVP PRINT, SALES & MARKETING: **DAVID GABRIEL**

BOOK DESIGNER: **RODOLFO MURAGUCHI**

EDITOR IN CHIEF: **C.B. CEBULSKI**

CHIEF CREATIVE OFFICER: **JOE QUESADA**

PRESIDENT: **DAN BUCKLEY**

EXECUTIVE PRODUCER: **ALAN FINE**

MILES MORALES: SPIDER-MAN VOL. 1 (SCHOLASTIC EDITION). Contains material originally published in magazine form as ULTIMATE COMICS SPIDER-MAN #1-5 and ULTIMATE COMICS FALLOUT #4. Second printing 2019. ISBN 978-1-302-91482-0. Published by MARVEL WORLDWIDE, INC., a subsidiary of MARVEL ENTERTAINMENT, LLC. OFFICE OF PUBLICATION: 135 West 50th Street, New York, NY 10020. Copyright © 2018 MARVEL No similarity between any of the names, characters, persons, and/or institutions in this magazine with those of any living or dead person or institution is intended, and any such similarity which may exist is purely coincidental. **Printed in Canada.** DAN BUCKLEY, President, Marvel Entertainment; JOHN NEE, Publisher; JOE QUESADA, Chief Creative Officer; TOM BREVOORT, SVP of Publishing; DAVID BOGART, SVP of Business Affairs & Operations, Publishing & Partnership; DAVID GABRIEL, SVP of Sales & Marketing, Publishing; JEFF YOUNGQUIST, VP of Production & Special Projects; DAN CARR, Executive Director of Publishing Technology; ALEX MORALES, Director of Publishing Operations; DAN EDINGTON, Managing Editor; SUSAN CRESPI, Production Manager; STAN LEE, Chairman Emeritus. For information regarding advertising in Marvel Comics or on Marvel.com, please contact Vit DeBellis, Custom Solutions & Integrated Advertising Manager, at vdebellis@marvel.com. For Marvel subscription inquiries, please call 888-511-5480. **Manufactured between 11/1/2018 and 12/3/2018 by SOLISCO PRINTERS, SCOTT, QC, CANADA.**

10 9 8 7 6 5 4 3 2

1

Because you were kind enough to sign all of my nondisclosure agreements and because you were curious enough to come here and pursue your very specific line of scientific expertise...

You will now learn one of the great secrets of the scientific community.

I created Spider-Man.

One of our original test subject spiders was genetically altered using an earlier version of my super-soldier Oz formula.

That spider bit a young man and that young man not only survived but was given the proportionate strength and abilities of that spider.

What?

You heard me.

And you don't know--wow, you don't know the specifications of the spider?

No. It died.

Do you have a log of the measurements of the formula that altered the spider?

I thought I did but no.

Can we get blood samples of the boy?

We have them.

And you weren't able to reverse-calculate the--?

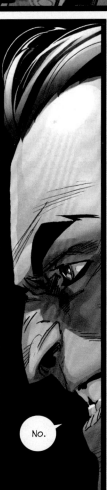

No.

But now we have *you!!*

And now I know why you were so crazy to buy out my contract from the Roxxon Corporation.

You're the expert in the field, Doctor Markus.

SLAP

Actually Otto Octavius is the real expert in the--

We don't talk about *that* man in *this* laboratory.

I said I will beat you to death with my bare hands.

You have four doctorates... which one of those words do you not understand?

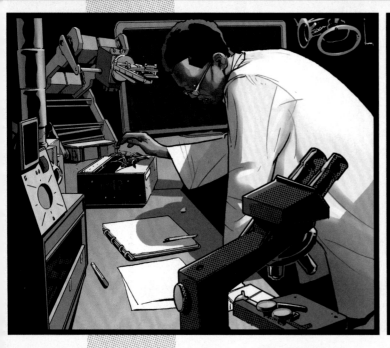

You *created* Spider-Man.

And I hope you understand that if this information leaves this building I will *kill* you.

Excuse me?

But if you solve this problem for me I will reward you to the point where I reinvent your life on every conceivable level.

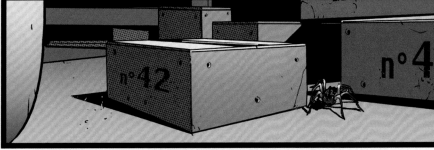

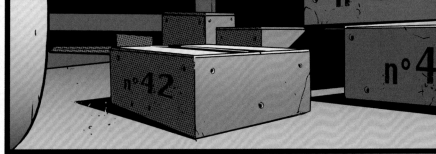

DAILY BUGLE

LOCAL | INTERNATIONAL | ARTS & ENTERTAINMENT | OPINION | SPORTS

NORMAN OSBORN IS THE GREEN GOBLIN!

CONTROVERSIAL INDUSTRIALIST IS REVEALED TO BE GENETICALLY ALTERED MONSTER NOW IN THE CUSTODY OF S.H.I.E.L.D.

Reporting by Frederick Fosswell

Agents of the world peacekeeping task force S.H.I.E.L.D. have confirmed to the Daily Bugle that controversial industrialist Norman Osborn had infected his own body with one of his experiments altering himself into what one of our S.H.I.E.L.D. sources are referring to as the Green Goblin.

Sources also confirm that this Green Goblin is the same one that attacked Midtown High School a few months ago, shutting the school down for weeks. It is also referred to as the public debut of the mystery man called Spider-Man. Whether or not there is a connection between Spider-Man and Norman Osborn's double life has yet to be revealed.

Speculation continues as to why Norman Osborn would break one of the cardinal rules of science by experimenting on himself. Sources close to Norman say that certain pressures to create a workable version of his experimental "super-soldier" formula led him to use the formula on himself.

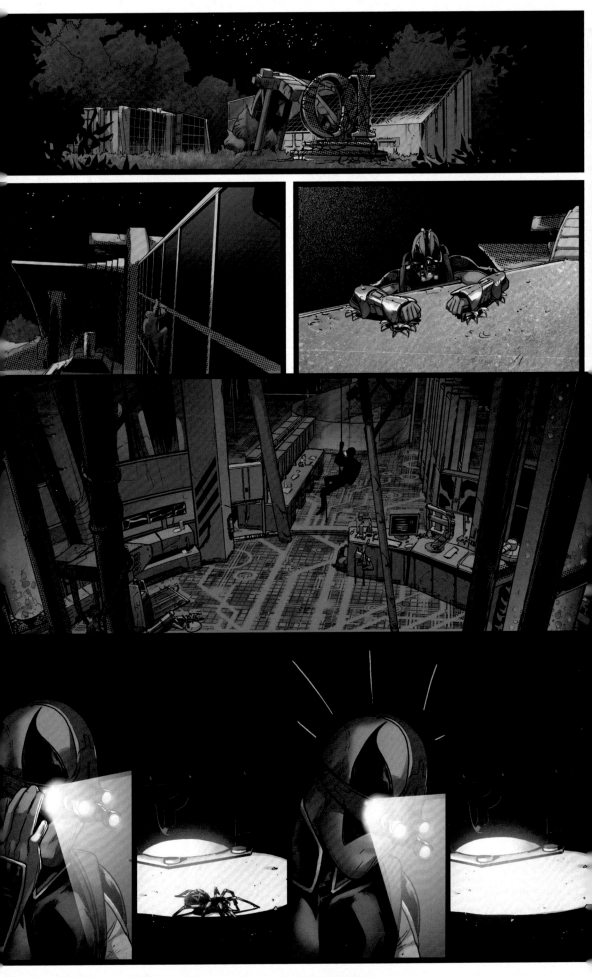

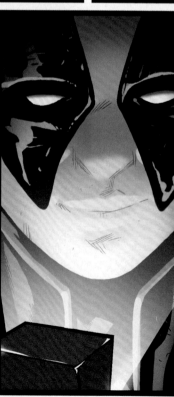

Brooklyn, New York.

This is a circus.

Stay focused, honey.

I am all focused.

It's just a damn circus.

You're making Miles nervous.

I'm fine.

Miles, baby, no matter what happens today... this is not a reflection on you.

This has nothing to do with you as a person.

There are only 40-some spots available in this charter school and there are, what? 700 applicants from our neighborhood.

I know.

I know.

You just need to stop and think about that.

It's just-- This is a lottery.

I know what a lottery is.

But it has nothing to do with you.

Please make this stop, Dad.

How long have you lived in our house?

Since birth.

And have I ever been able to make this stop?

I thought just this once.

Let's just get this foolishness over with.

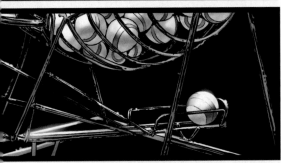

Miles Morales.

Get outta town.

Oh, my God.

Oh--oh-- you have a chance.

Oh, my God, you have a chance.

It's--it's all happening.

It shouldn't-- all these other kids.

Should it be like this?

Just focus on you. You got in. Focus on that.

You get to pick dinner, kid.

KNOCK KNOCK

Uncle Aaron, it's Miles!!

Uh, hold on!

There he is.

My man.

Hey, Uncle Aaron.

Get in here, boy.

How's your mom?

She's happy today.

Why's that?

I got into that charter school.

That's-- that's damn good news.

I didn't do anything, though. It was just a lottery.

No, no... you got your ticket out of this cesspool.

You play your cards right, you make your own way. Your dad and me didn't have a chance in that school we went to.

You did okay.

Listen to me...

This is a good thing. This-- this calls for popsicles.

Right?

Yeah.

Your daddy gonna be able to pay for it?

You make it.

Don't let people make it for you.

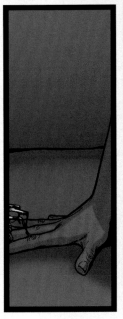

What's this?

Oh hey no. That is something else--that is something for work.

What is it?

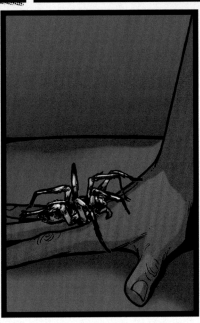

AGH!

What the--?!!

RASH!

What the hell happened? What the hell??

What-- hey--what happened?

Miles!

Miles??

Oh thank God! Are you *okay*?

What happened?

You fainted is what happened! I had to call your--

What the hell did you do!!

--father.

Are you okay?

Yeah, Dad. I just

What did he do to you?

What? No. I got bit by, like, a spider.

What did you give him?

What did you give him?

What??

A popsicle.

What the hell kind of guy you think I am??

I have no damn idea what kind of guy you are.

Dad, stop it.

2

Brooklyn, New York.

So I said to the guy: You never read the book yet you go online and talk about it as if--

Agh!

Whoa!

How did you--?

Damn!

How did you **do** that?

You shouldn't be *running in the street!!*

What the *wha-- hey?*

Whoa!

It was a-a-a mutant!!

It *was!!*

I hate this city.

A damn mutant!!

Oh, God--Oh, man--Oh, God--Oh, man--

This isn't happening.

Please tell me this isn't happening.

How is this *happening?*

@#$@#$!

What?

Little ##$@, just *zapped* me!!

With what

N-No, I didn't.

I was just playin'. But you go and pull some nasty--

Ggkkk!!

Whoa!!

Ggkkk!!

What just *happened*

Get away from me!!!

What the hell?

He's a--he's one of those *mutants!!*

Oh *damn!!*

We should call the police!!

Can't believe I'm seeing a real mutant.

I thought they were made up.

We should call the police.

And tell them *what?*

Thank God you're home.

Miles!! Dude!

I need you, Ganke. I need your brain.

Just let me finish the masthead.

I need you to come back to real life and I need you to help me.

What's going on?

What I am about to *say* and *show* you can *never* be talked about outside of *this room*.

I need you to *promise* me that what I'm about to say and show you will *never* be talked about outside of *this* room.

What *happened*?

I don't know what we're talking about.

Promise me.

Tell me what we're talking about.

Promise me.

Dude.

Have I ever, ever screwed you over?

You're the only person I *talk* to.

Who am I going to tell whatever you're about to say?

Okay, I want you to *watch* this.

Okay.

Prepare to be freaked out like you've never been freaked out *before*.

Please don't take off your pants.

Just watch.

Did it happen?

Just watch.

Where am I supposed to be looking at exactly?

Are you taking a dump?

It's not *cool* to give up any sense of a--A normal life.

You get to--

It's not *cool* to end up in a military *concentration camp* or something.

They don't put mutants in camps.

Yes, they do.

That's all, like, a conspi--

A mutant *drowned* this city.

You do not get to be a *mutant* in New York City!!

Okay, okay.

You can't tell anybody about this.

Hold on, roll back... a spider bit you? A spider with a *number*?

What number?

You can't tell anyone.

We have to figure out how your powers work.

I don't have *powers*.

Dude, *you* have powers.

And I don't care what you say: this is insanely cool.

I'm scared out of my mind.

Son. Let's go.

I didn't even know he was here in our house.

Let's *go*!

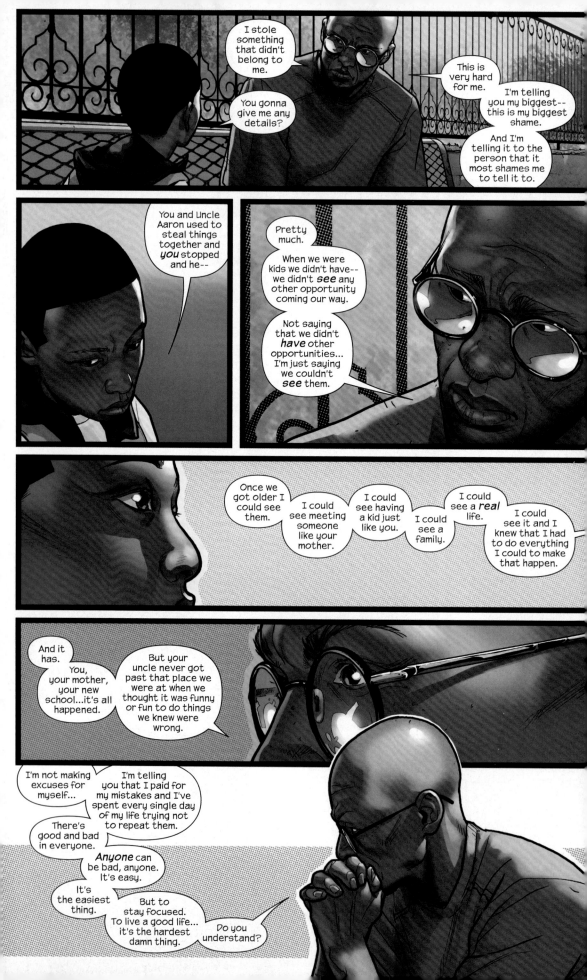

Ganke THE AWESOME:
today, 1:07 am

you're not a mutant.

Ganke THE AWESOME:
today, 1:07 am

you're not a mutant.

Ganke THE AWESOME:
today, 1:08 am

u have chameleon like powers like some spiders do- & u have a venom strike, like some spiders have.

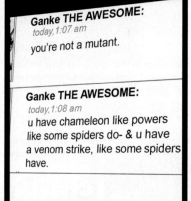

u have chameleon like powers like some spiders do- & u have a venom strike, like some spiders have.

Sir MILES:
today, 1:09 am

what r u talking about?

today, 1:09 am

what r u talking about?

Ganke THE AWESOME:
today, 1:10 am

Spider-Man was bit by a spider too.

Spider-man was bit by a spide too.

Ganke THE AWESOME:
today,1:12 am
Spider-Man myth busted By Ben Urich

Ganke THE AWESOME:
today,1:12 am
Sp myth busted By

HOW SPIDER-MAN BECAME SPIDER-MAN
By BEN URICH
picture by Peter Parker

though said with levity, Spider-Man told police officers that he was bit by a spider that gave him spider-powers.

STARPICS
Z100

Ganke THE AWESOME:
today,1:10 am
sorry u'r not a mutant but...
R U Spider-Man?!!

Ganke THE AWES
today,1:10 am
sorry u'r not a mut
R U Spider-Man?!

3

KNOCK
KNOCK

Uncle Aaron, it's Miles!!

He's not home.

Uncle Aaron?

We have to, like, test your powers.

You're not dying.

I should go to a doctor. I could be dying.

Hey, can you make webs?

Webs?

Spider-Man makes webs!

Do they come out of his body or does he have a--?

WEEEEOOOOOOWWWEEEOOOOOHONKHON

WEEEEOOOOOOWWWEEEOOOOOHONKHON

Whoa!

Ho!

Hi.

Uh, take my hand.

Aaaaiiiee!!

Yeah, uh, please.

What the hey?

WhatamI doing?WhatamI doing?Whatam Idoing?

Get aiaaway from me!! Don't touch me!!

HELLO! I'm trying to save your--

AAIIEE STOPWHAT AREYOU--??!

Sorry!

AAIIEESTOP WHATAREYOU DOOIIINNGG??!

Woof!

Ruff!

FUMP

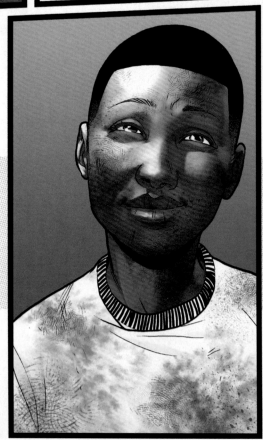

That was *amazing!!*

Are you okay?

Kaff!! C-can't breathe good.

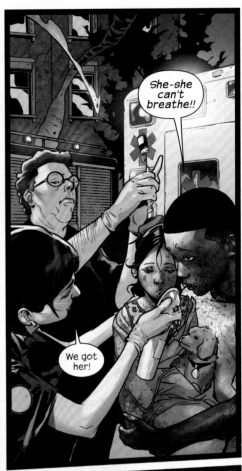

She-she can't breathe!!

We got her!

Kid, that was *amazing!!* Crazy but amazing.

You okay??

How did you *do* that??

What's your name?

Told you Spider-Man was black.

Miles?

Miles!!

HUUAAGG!!

Ughhhh!

Dude, that was *amazing*.

HUUAAGG!!

Dude, huh?

Hey hey...

What was I *doing*?

You saved those people.

I've never- I've never done anything like that before *in my life.*

You never had spider-powers before.

You know what I mean.

Welcome to the Brooklyn Visions Academy.

I can see from the look in your eyes how excited you are.

And I know that for some of you this is your f night away fro home.

Hey

Hey...

They said this is my room too.

Welcome.

Do you have superpowers too?

My name is Judge.

Ganke. This is Miles.

If you wanted the top bunk you should've got here sooner.

That's a'ight.

I like this guy.

Easy going.

"And I can promise you that you will be given the tools and the techniques you'll need to make these dreams come true.

...nd some you are a ...le scared.

This is your kingdom.

You have nothing to be afraid of. This is the safest place on earth.

But you get to see your family on the weekends and, trust me, in just a couple of weeks you will be fully integrated into this new lifestyle of yours.

It is a lifestyle of learning.

It is a lifestyle of imagination.

Of community.

Of purpose.

You guys seem normal. Huge relief.

What are your feelings on Legos?

Legos are dope.

I *like* this guy!!

I know that many of you are very goal oriented towards your future--and that's good.

We encourage that.

That's why we frown on a lot of internet surfing and outside distraction.

"Here you get to learn, excel, explore your mind.

"You get to discover what you can really do."

Nugaagh!!

S'goinon...

Nothin' m'ok!

Whoa!

What are you doing?? Stop it!!

Everybody out of bed!! Emergency drill!!

Is there a fire?

Leave your stuff and follow everyone into the gymnasium.

Let's go let's go!!

Okay, okay...

Everybody calm down.

Everything is going to be okay.

We have a city-mandated regulation emergency drill every time there is *any sort* of unusual superpowered activity in the city.

What's going on?

We don't have all the information but there is some sort of super hero war zone happening on the Queensboro Bridge.

The news has reported that there have been some fatalities...

This is going on *right now*?

Everything's going to be okay.

Again, I don't know all the details but...

Supposedly...

Who got hurt?

4

Please, please...

Everybody calm down.

Everything is going to be okay.

You said Spider-Man's been shot and the city's *gone crazy!!*

How is that okay?

I told you we don't have all the information, Ganke.

I told you what is on the news.

We have a city mandate to gather you in drill formation and wait for further instruction.

Can I call my mom?

We are already in the process of calling your parents.

Cover for me.

Just-- please, Ganke.

Miles?

Cover.

Cover?

What are you going to do?

I will destroy your family like you destroyed mine!! I will kill everyone you know!!

Could you do it--

Quietly?!

SMASH

There you go.

Ow!

What? Instead of being a coward.

How was this at all--??

You know I could have helped stop this.

I would have used my powers when I first got them--

Like I was *supposed* to--

Like you *told* me to--

If I wouldn't have been *hiding* in this room...then by now my whole life would've been different.

I-I would've met Spider-Man.

I would've been in--in the loop.

I would've known what was going on and I would've been able to help.

Loop?

Maybe--

Yes! I would have been the extra something that *stopped* this from happening.

Maybe.

Or maybe you would've gotten killed too.

I was given these powers for a reason.

You said it.

And I sit here...scared of my dad...

I'm scared of everything...

And now look at what's happened!!

Or Maybe--

Maybe *this* is what you were given the powers for.

Maybe you're supposed to be Spider-Man now that we don't have one anymore.

Maybe you're the Spider-Man in the on-deck circle...and now it's your turn.

This is crazy.

All the bridges are closed.

You think we'll get the day off school?

What?

The Funeral of Peter Parker.

Excuse us.

Sorry.

Excuse me.

Are you Spider-Man's mommy?

Uh-oh.

Because his uncle, the guy who raised him, died.

Peter thought he died because even though he had these powers he didn't do anything to help.

'Least that's the way Peter saw it.

And his uncle told him these words, words he lived by:

That with great power comes great responsibility.

Okay?

Wow.

Dude.

Why'd he wear a mask though?

Because he didn't need anyone to know who he was to be a hero.

And it looked @#$¢ cool.

HA HA HAAA!!!

Oh my God!!

What was I waiting for!!??

This is amazing!!

This is-- oh man!!

Okay, okay...

Big question!!

Now how am I supposed to sit in class all day when I know I can--

CRAASH

Crash??

ACT *SCRATCH MATCH*

You want to tell me that again?!!

I get out of prison and you tell me you *"lost"* my cut of our last job??

Please, come on, Kangaroo, you didn't give me a--

Don't speak to me like you *know me!!*

I only want one thing--!!

Give me what you owe me.

Or I will beat you to death.

Wow.

That ain't nice at all.

CRASH

Ow.

That is in *terrible* taste.

I-I thought you died.

Really.

Now I'm gonna smell like pizza for a week.

Does *everyone* in this city have powers?

Did he *actually* call himself the Kangaroo?

Why would someone call himself the--?

YOW!

BOOM

SMACK

Did you--

The buzzing again.

SMAAASSHH

DAILY ◆ BUGLE

News
games - scores - lotteries

Gossip
video - photos - blogs

Sports
subscribe

Life
NYC Local — Bus

Gord has tentative deal with TWR

SPIDER-MAN NO MORE... PLEASE!!

COPYCAT HERO RIPS UP CITY

By Frederick Foswell-reporter

"It really was in bad taste."
Was the opinion of one of the dozens of New Yorkers who were witness to the calamitous debut of a young man who took it upon himself to dress as Spider-Man and take to the night.

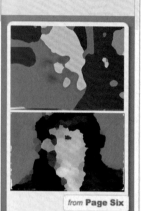

from **Page Six**

Though he was victorious in a powered street fight with a career criminal who calls himself the Kangaroo, witnesses say that his lack of skill and naivete made the battle a clumsy dance of

Maybe it *was* in bad taste.

Ya think?

Wow, the Bugle is really dumping on you.

Really?

Uh, really.

I thought they *loved* Spider-Man.

I remember they used to dump on him too.

I just thought I'd get a chance to--

THUMP THUMP

Uh-oh.

THUMP THUMP

Guys!!

Why are you locking the door?? Hello?? I heard you in there!!

Sorry about that.

Why did you lock the door?

I didn't. It must've locked itself. Can I come into my room?

Hey, I forgot to ask, did you do the calculus--?

Let me in!!

What's going on?

Nothing.

You don't lock the doors.

I didn't. I-It was stuck on a--

I mean it.

Yes sir.

Sir.

What's going on in here??

Reading.

Why? Whassup?

The door doesn't lock. It's against school rules and it's a fire hazard.

Okay.

You guys are pals and we let you room together.

Don't make us rethink it.

It was an accident.

What's *your* deal?

Tired.

This is not going to work.

How did you do it, Peter?

Well, you probably didn't live in a shoebox dormitory.

Okay, I need more practice. I need to come up with a plan.

Why am I talking to myself all of a sudden?

5

Just a kid.

We were all kids once.

When I was a kid I stayed home and watched TV.

Whatzz?

I invented cellular technology.

Is that true?

Wow. He *is* just a kid.

Oh man...

It's not the *kid* part that bothers me.

It's the Spider-Man part.

The outfit *is* in bad taste, young man.

Mister Morales, welcome to...

The Triskelion- Ultimates Headquarters.

You--you--I didn't--oh boy.

I didn't *do* anything!!

What *did* he do?

Hello? *Look* at him!

Not exactly a federal offense.

We can't have *that* happening.

His blood work is back.

The kid's the real deal.

Is he a mutant?

No. Just--hmm.

Nope.

Just altered.

Not unlike you and *very* like Peter Parker.

What does that mean?

(God rest his soul.)

What does *that* mean?

Another one?

Did you try asking *him*?

Yes!

Before or after you hit him?

How can *this* be??

Well--

What does that mean?

Everybody out.

I'd like to stay.

You can write about the disappointment in your blog.

Out.

What does this mean?

Another one.

Hello, Miles.

How--

Do we know your name?

We've got all kinds of ways to find *that* out.

My name is Nick Fury.

How did you get your powers?

I--I get a phone call or something.

You're not under arrest. We're just talkin'.

This-- this feels like under arrest.

Settle down.

You put on that costume, you have to pay the price.

The price is--people get upset.

You get that, right?

Quite a rap sheet on that uncle of yours.

The FBI calls him *The Prowler.*

(I didn't know that.)

I didn't think so.

Do your parents know about your... spiderness?

No.

And you don't want them to?

No-- no, not yet.

ZZZZZT!

Why the costume?

The other one--the other Spider-Man died.

I thought--

I felt--

That with great power.

Comes-- yeah.

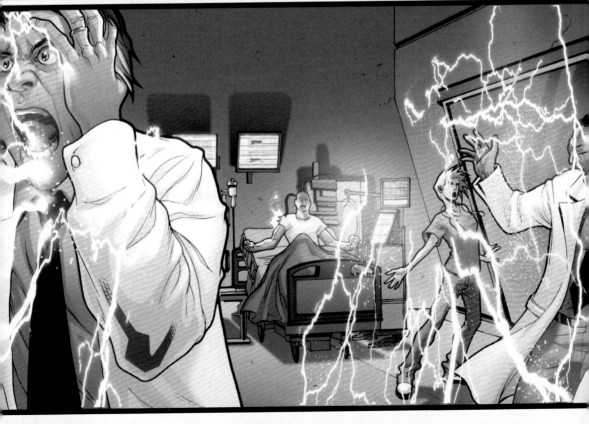

CRASH

What's happening, soldier?

Prison break. Maxwell Dillon.

Which one *is* that?

Electro, Sir.

You stay with me.

A-team, *top side!!*

Hey there, Sparky.

How far did you think you'd get? I mean *really.*

Don't even know *you* are.

Everybody take cover!!

SHUT THE PERIMETER!!

Take cover if you're not equipped!!

Heeeeey, eye patch!

EVERYONE OUT!!

Take cover!!

BAM BAM BAM

Yeah?

Tried to ruin my life, Fury, huh?

Guess it's my turn.

FSSHH

FSSHH

FSSHH

And I *know* I should just leave, but the chance to fry you to ash is just *too* yummy.

Kid, run--

I would really *love* to hear you scream.

Huh.

BOOM

"That did *not* happen."

"It all did."

"You *beat* Electro."

"Is that his name?"

"How? What did you do?"

That thing--when I punch someone--that little ZZT.

Your venom blast.

Whatever.

It disrupted his thingamabob.

Did you know it would *do* that?

I thought *maybe*--and I had to try something.

Dude. *Dude, you're a super hero!!*

Oh my God!!

Sshh!!

Sorry.

Shh!

Shh!!

Nick *Fury,* man!!

And he just let you go home?

They had a big mess to clean up and I had to get back here.

What did he say?

He said he had to think about me.

What does that mean?

Dude, I'm still freaked out about the girl with the--

Miles.

Uh, do I know you?

We met earlier. Up there.

Oh.

Oh?

She's-- you're--

Here.

It's from Fury.

He said you get one chance.

He said you were getting no chances but yesterday you bought yourself one chance.

This--this isn't a joke to me or a kid's game.

This is--it's everything.

You put that on.

You make yourself a part of this.

It means you're representing-- it means--

You get it.

I do.

Sorry I got rough with you.

This is all just-- it's uncharted territory for me.

This is mine?

See you around, Miles.

Do you know what this means?

Whoa.

It means you're talking to girls now.

It means I have to start talking to girls.

Oh, dude...

That's cool.

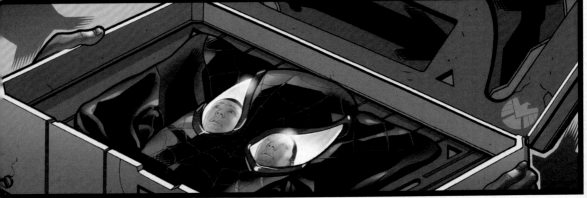

#1 VARIANT
BY SARA PICHELLI & JUSTIN PONSOR

#1 SKETCH VARIANT
BY SARA PICHELLI

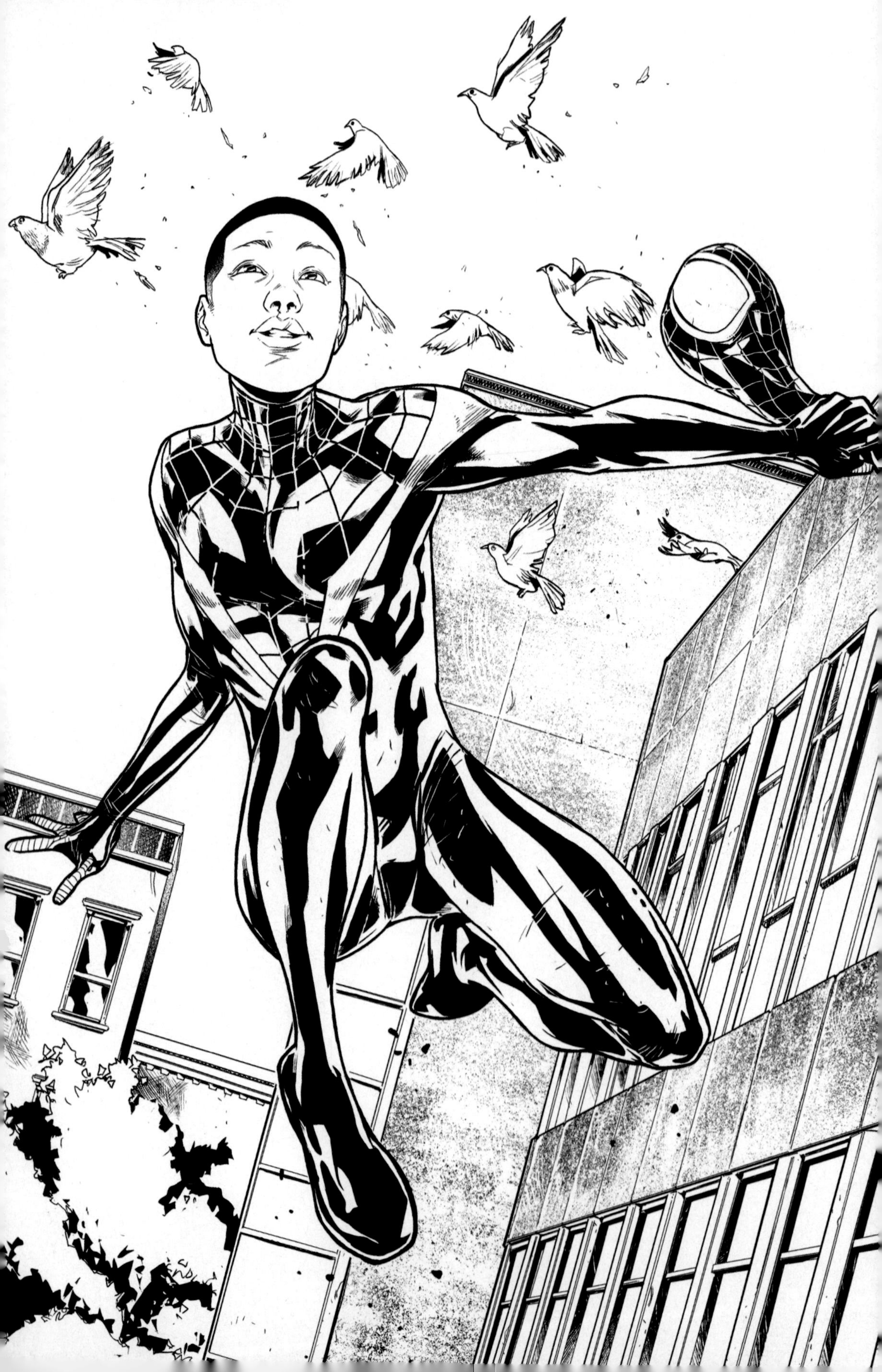

No.

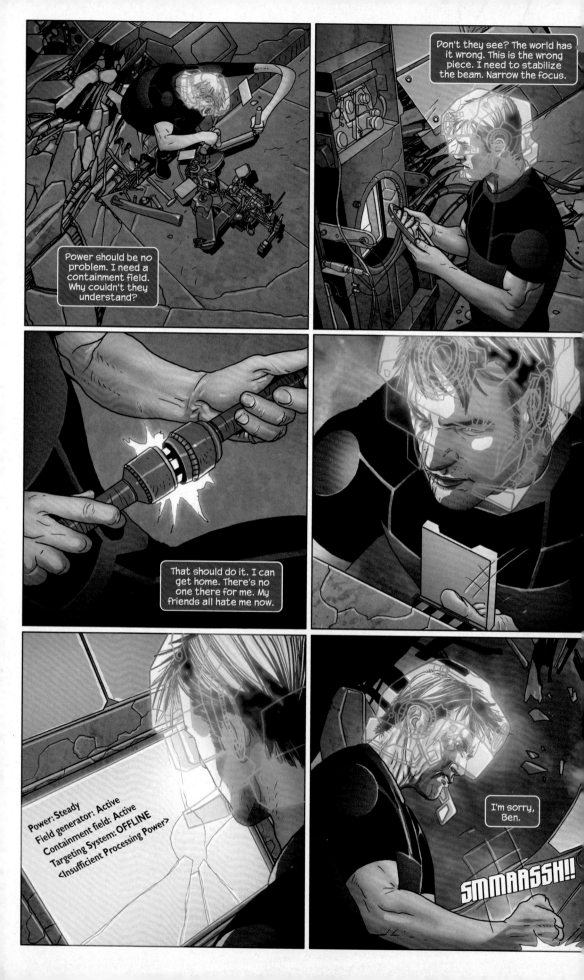

ZZZAKKKK

I'm going
to solve
everything.

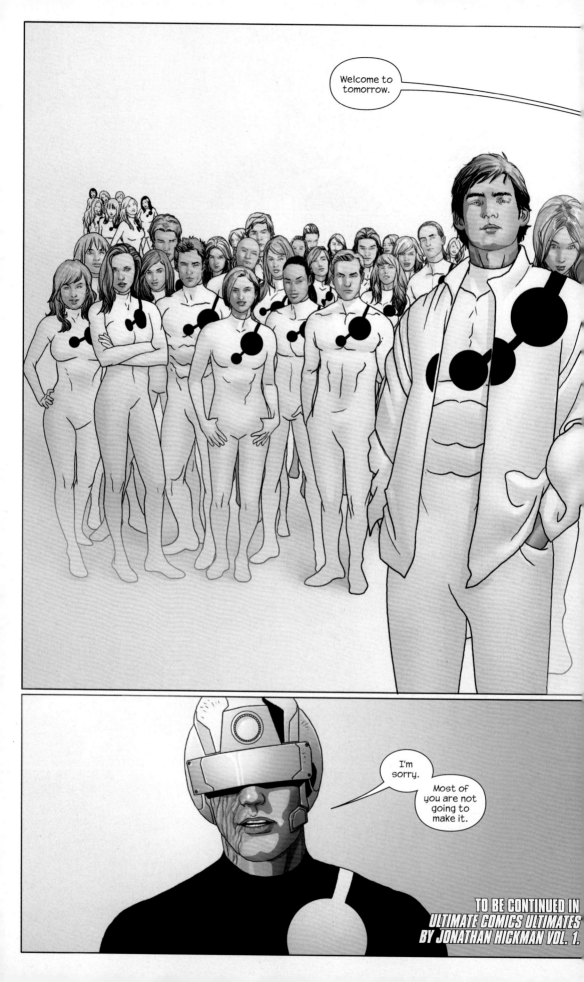

Maybe in a minute.

I was in *Vancouver* over the weekend, Val.

So is *this* why we're getting coffee? You want an interview with *Captain America*? He's not gonna want to talk about this Spider-kid thing.

Can you believe they film all those TV shows there? It doesn't look *anything* like New York.

Hm. No. There was an old man living up there, *burn victim*. Really ghastly. Just got diagnosed with terminal cancer, said he wanted to get his story out before he passed. Said he's tired of lying to the grandkids.

This some kind of human interest thing? I didn't know you had a soul. *Seriously,* you should try this--

He also happens to be a *mutant*. And he says he spent a bunch of years locked in a government research facility, getting experimented on.

Black Helicopters.

You know that saying comes from the fact that there were black helicopters, right?

Come on, Brett, you know how it was back then. It was the Wild West. Everyone was poking and prodding mutants.

Yeah, but the timestamp on this stuff is *way* earlier. Like, *the earliest.*

Well everybody's gotta go to the prom *sometime,* I guess. So, *what,* you're running this? Cold War-era mutant testing? And you wonder why your demos are aging.

It's *Valerie Cooper*. Where is he?

Well, *pull him out of it*. Get him on the phone with the Attorney General--there's going to be an independent counsel on this, we need to be ready. And C.O.S. needs to start calling the governors, we want all national guard units on alert. *Then*--

Shut up, let me finish--we need the networks, no later than *eight*. Phil's gonna have to work something up--"what began as a noble *experiment*, words cannot express, full responsibility, *violence* is not the answer"--

Would you just do what I *tell* you to, damn it?!! Listen to me--we're three hours away from half this country going up in flames. There's gonna be *riots* coast to coast, and that's not even *touching* the international response--

The entire world's about to find out The United States government created mutants.

TO BE CONTINUED IN
ULTIMATE COMICS X-MEN BY NICK SPENCER VOL. 1.